IR

DISCARD

WILD WHEELS

GTOs

By Heather Moore Niver

Gareth Stevens
Publishing

Please visit our Web site, www.garethstevens.com. For a free color catalog of all our high-quality books, call toll free 1-800-542-2595 or fax 1-877-542-2596.

Library of Congress Cataloging-in-Publication Data

Niver, Heather Moore.
 GTOs / Heather Moore Niver.
   p. cm. – (Wild wheels)
 Includes index.
 ISBN 978-1-4339-4748-3 (pbk.)
 ISBN 978-1-4339-4749-0 (6-pack)
 ISBN 978-1-4339-4747-6 (library binding)
 1. GTO automobile—Juvenile literature. I. Title.
 TL215.G79N58 2011
 629.222'2–dc22

                                        2010037589

First Edition

Published in 2011 by
Gareth Stevens Publishing
111 East 14th Street, Suite 349
New York, NY 10003

Copyright © 2011 Gareth Stevens Publishing

Designer: Christopher Logan
Editor: Therese Shea

Photo credits: Cover, p. 1 (car and background), pp. 2–3, 30–32 (background), 2–32 (flame border), back cover (engine), 22–23, 26–27 Shutterstock.com; pp. 4, 5, 6–7, 8–9, 16–17, 18–19, 20–21, 24–25, 28–29, © Kimball Stock Photo; pp. 10–11 Franko Lee/AFP/Getty Images; pp. 12, 15 © Frank Melling; p. 13 Mark Thompson/Getty Images.

Printed in the United States of America

CPSIA compliance information: Batch #CW11GS: For further information contact Gareth Stevens, New York, New York at 1-800-542-2595.

CONTENTS

Words in the glossary appear in **bold** type the first time they are used in the text.

Go, Go, GTO!

Italian, Japanese, American, and South African companies have all made GTOs. There's even a GTO motorcycle! No matter how many wheels it has or where it's made, the GTO goes fast!

Ferrari is the Italian company that made the first GTO car in the early 1960s. "GTO" stands for "Gran Turismo Omologato," which is Italian for "Grand Touring Homologated." The approval of a car for racing is called "homologation." To enter the GT racing class, Ferrari had to produce at least 100 high-performance sports cars for street driving.

1962 Ferrari 250 GTO

Ferrari only built **39 GTOs**, not the **100** cars the race rules required. To be allowed to race, Ferrari argued that its **250 GTO** model was similar to another car it was already selling—the **250 GT**. The race committee agreed. The Ferrari **250 GTO** won the International Championship for **GT Manufacturers** in 1962, 1963, and 1964.

The Ferrari GTO was only sold as a street car so that it could race against other high-performance sports cars.

Ferrari's GTOs

Ferrari paid careful attention to every detail of their 250 GTO. The body shape was planned by a group of specialists. It was tested on a racetrack and even in a **wind tunnel**. On the inside, only the most important features were included. The 250 GTO didn't even have a **speedometer**!

In 2004, the 250 GTO was named one of the Top Sports Cars of All Time by *Sports Car International*.

Some car fans say that the 250 GTO is the greatest sports car ever. *Motor Trend Classic* magazine called the 250 GTO the greatest Ferrari of all time. "It's the car we dreamed about as kids," said one of the voters, an employee of Ford Motor Company.

INSIDE THE MACHINE

Mauro Forghieri is one of the great Ferrari designers. He started out working in the company's engine department. The next year, he advanced to the job of chief engineer. Forghieri helped create the 250 GTO as well as other sporty Ferraris.

In 1984, the second Ferrari GTO—the 288—burst onto the car scene. The biggest advancement from other Ferrari road cars was the strong, light body. It was 700 pounds (318 kg) lighter than similar models!

Ferrari made this GTO to race, just like the 250 GTO. The car, tested by *Automobile Revue*, reached 62 miles (100 km) per hour in just 4.8 seconds. It reached a top speed of 180 miles (290 km) per hour. Unfortunately, a race scheduled to show off the car never happened due to track safety issues.

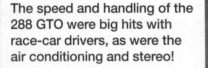

The speed and handling of the 288 GTO were big hits with race-car drivers, as were the air conditioning and stereo!

INSIDE THE MACHINE

The 288 was named for its 2.8-liter engine with eight cylinders, also called a V-8. It may not have raced, but Ferrari couldn't make enough 288 GTOs to satisfy eager car fans! The company had to increase production from 200 to 272 to meet demands.

When Ferrari unveiled its 2011 599 GTO, it announced that it was the fastest car on the road! With a powerful engine, the car could zoom from 0 to 60 miles (97 km) per hour in just 3.35 seconds. In tests, it reached a top speed of 208 miles (335 km) per hour! A car that fast has to stop quickly, so the 599 has light, high-performance brakes.

The 599 GTO is Ferrari's fastest road car yet. Maybe it's the fastest because it was based on the racetrack model—the 599XX. Like the other Ferrari GTOs, the company only made a limited number. The number decided upon was 599.

INSIDE THE MACHINE

Sports cars must be in control. Normally, the weight of a car is the only thing that forces the tires down. Fast turns can be very dangerous. The Ferrari has a small rear spoiler to increase its grip on the road. The spoiler uses wind to generate force to keep the car from tipping over.

The 599 GTO wowed crowds at the Beijing Auto Show in April 2010.

GTO on Two Wheels

Most GTOs are cars, but not all of them! The Bridgestone Corporation started out making bicycles with motors to sell in the United States to compete with the Honda Motor Company. Soon they started manufacturing more powerful motorcycles, too. Among Bridgestone's bikes was the 1967 350 GTO. The 350 GTO motorcycle was modeled after the 350 GTR. "GTR" stands for "Grand Turismo Racing." This GTO motorcycle had a quiet, air-cooled engine designed to make room for an **alternator**.

The 350 GTO even had a built-in toolbox!

The bike was stylish. With a specially painted, shining frame, the GTO cycle turned heads! Some fans say that the 350 GTO motorcycle was the best bike of its time.

INSIDE THE MACHINE

Bridgestone didn't make many GTO motorcycles. Production occurred in the same factories as the Bridgestone tires. Also, the high-quality parts needed to make the motorcycles were very expensive. Since producing only a small number of bikes didn't make much of a profit, the product was discontinued.

The main difference between the GTR and the GTO was the GTO's higher-mounted **exhaust** pipe. This newer bike was marketed as a "scrambler," meaning it could be driven on or off the road. Some road bikes can be altered to be scramblers, too. This was a bonus for riders who liked to explore trails and rough roads. Some scrambler fans weren't sure that this minor change to the exhaust pipe could turn a road bike into a true off-road bike. Still, the GTO's on-road performance made it an instant classic.

Since few of these motorcycles were made, they're quite rare today. Even when they were on the market, Bridgestone only had a few dealers.

INSIDE THE MACHINE

Bridgestone stopped making motorcycles in the late 1960s. They focused on manufacturing tires. Some said that the company realized they could make a lot more money by selling tires to all the other car and motorcycle companies. Today, Bridgestone tires are well known.

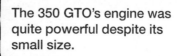
The 350 GTO's engine was quite powerful despite its small size.

Mitsubishi GTO

The Japanese company Mitsubishi produced its first Galant GTO (or Colt Galant GTO) in 1970. It had an eye-catching look with a combination of three striking features. First, it had a "dyna-wedge" body, meaning it was **aerodynamic** and streamlined. Second, it had a "ducktail" rear, similar to the shape of a duck's upturned tail. Third, the GTO had the long hood of a traditional **pony car**. A new Saturn-brand engine gave it power.

The 1975 Galant GTO featured Mitsubishi Silent Shaft technology. This made the engine run smoothly and quietly. Other automobile companies liked this technology so much that they paid Mitsubishi to use it, too.

INSIDE THE MACHINE

The original Mitsubishi GTO was designed by Hiroaki Kamisago. The company sent him to study at the Art Center College of Design in Pasadena, California. The car's style honored many American muscle cars of the time, such as the Ford Mustang and Pontiac Firebird.

The Mitsubishi spoiler works like an upside down airplane wing. Instead of making upward force like a wing, it makes downward force.

17

Mitsubishi didn't produce another GTO again until the early 1990s. It developed a stylish sports **coupe** to compete with cars such as the Mazda RX-7, Nissan 300ZX, and Toyota Supra. The 3000GT's front and rear spoilers lengthened and withdrew, depending on the car's speed. **All-wheel drive** made the driver confident on the road when driving fast. The car also had very tough brakes.

Unfortunately, all these features made the Mitsubishi GTO heavier than its rivals. In addition, some complained that it wasn't large enough to allow tall people to sit up straight! The last of these fast, good-looking cars was made in 1999.

INSIDE THE MACHINE

Mitsubishi's **GTO** was known as a **Mitsubishi 3000GT** in every country except Japan. Mitsubishi was concerned that car experts wouldn't like the GTO name on a Japanese car. No matter what the model was called, every car was built at Mitsubishi's plant in Nagoya, Japan.

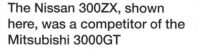

The Nissan 300ZX, shown here, was a competitor of the Mitsubishi 3000GT

19

Pontiac Muscles In

Pontiac is a brand in the General Motors (GM) car family. Some car fans say that 1964 was the beginning of the muscle-car age. That was the year John DeLorean first issued the Pontiac GTO.

The Pontiac GTO had a lot of attitude! It had a powerful engine and rumbling dual exhausts. It also had a hood scoop. A scoop is a raised part on the hood that increases airflow to the engine to boost power. However, the GTO hood scoop was fake! It was added to make the car look tougher.

Ferrari fans were shocked that Pontiac took the name of their beloved sports car! But General Motors believed its new Pontiac was sporty and powerful enough to use the GTO name.

INSIDE THE MACHINE

John DeLorean is best known as the father of the GTO. He put the V-8 engine in the Pontiac LeMans to create an upscale GTO. DeLorean is also praised for keeping the company on the cutting edge. After leaving Pontiac, he started his own company.

For the first 10 years of production, Pontiac used a platform (or size, power, and design) called an "A-body." Lots of GM cars used this platform. On the GTO Tempest, buyers could choose the powerful V-8 engine for an extra speedy ride.

A special 1969 Pontiac GTO was known as "The Judge." The name was based on a popular line from comedian Sammy Davis Jr.: "Here comes the judge!" The car was expensive and looked forceful. It had a black **grille**, spoiler, stripes, and stickers that said "The Judge." People didn't need to be told when this Judge was coming!

The Judge was an option package for the 1969 GTO. An option package is a list of features added to a regular car model.

INSIDE THE MACHINE

Every year, Pontiac updated the GTO. This made buyers keep an eye on changes. For example, the 1968 GTO had an Endura bumper. It was rubber and made the car look as if it didn't even have a bumper. It was so strong that TV ads showed John DeLorean pounding it with a hammer!

23

In 1970, the Judge was given a new front-end style and offered as a coupe or **convertible**. But the Judge's rule was almost over. The government passed laws that were good for the environment, but not so good for the GTO. Sales of the Judge and other GTOs began to fall.

In 1973 and 1974, the GTO was just an option package on other models. The Endura bumper was replaced with a steel one. The car may have been a looker on the outside, but inside everything was very simple. The instrument panel was very basic, and the seats were plain. This was a big change from earlier GTOs.

Options are choices. There are many options when it comes to buying a car. Back in the 1970s, options included features such as leather seats, kind of engine (such as the V-8), and striped hoods. Today's options include top-of-the-line stereos, navigation systems, and even televisions.

The Judge had dual hood scoops to cool the engine.

It was another 30 years before GTOs were back on the highway. Pontiac showed some **concept cars**, but none of them ever hit the pavement. Finally, in 2004, Pontiac developed another GTO model—the Monaro. This GTO was a big change from earlier models. It was the first GTO without a fake hood scoop, and it was the quickest yet.

The 2005 and 2006 GTOs were even speedier, thanks to their V-8 engines. They could drive 1/4 mile (400 m) in 13.5 seconds! However, the high price tag was a factor in making the 2006 the last model year of this pony car.

The Pontiac GTO was nicknamed "the Goat" by some of its drivers.

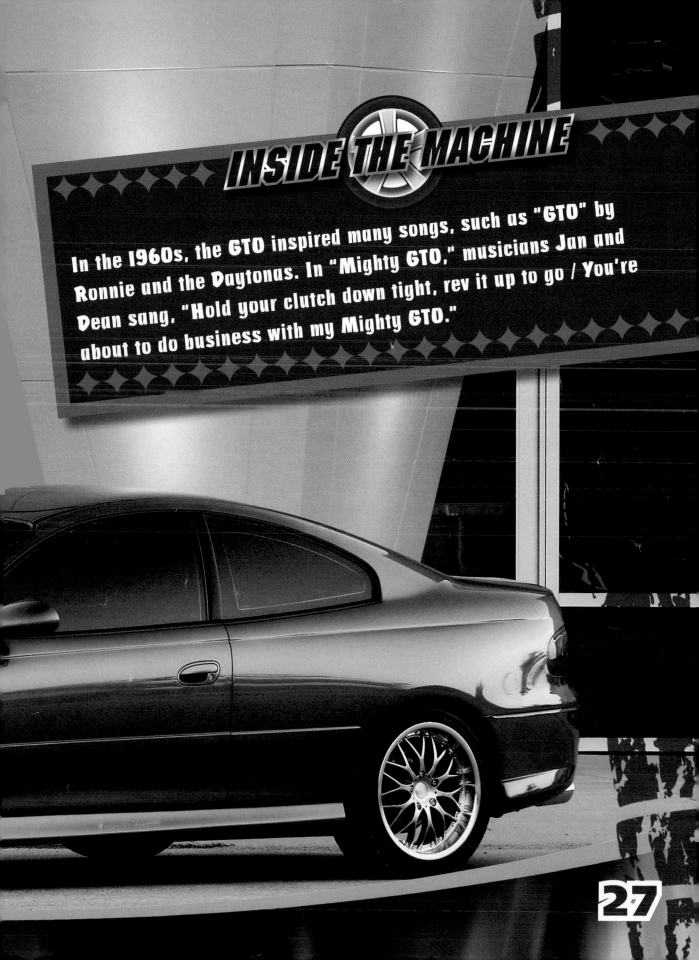

INSIDE THE MACHINE

In the 1960s, the GTO inspired many songs, such as "GTO" by Ronnie and the Daytonas. In "Mighty GTO," musicians Jan and Dean sang, "Hold your clutch down tight, rev it up to go / You're about to do business with my Mighty GTO."

Noble GTO

In 2005, car designer and race-car driver Lee Noble built the Noble M12 GTO in South Africa. It zips 1/4 mile (400 m) in only 11.8 seconds. It can reach 60 miles (97 km) in a blazing 3.3 seconds. The Noble GTO is a rare "goat," but it's a fast looker!

No matter who makes it, the stylish and speedy GTO is a lasting name. It has burned rubber on four wheels and two. The GTO has been a constant favorite of many car lovers and motorcycle fans around the world since the first one hit the pavement.

INSIDE THE MACHINE

The Noble M12 GTO is called a "kit" or "component car." This means that it arrives in two pieces. One crate holds the already assembled car. The parts that carry the engine's power to the wheels (called the power train) are in the other box. It takes about **40** hours to put everything together.

Few cars in the world can reach high speeds as quickly as a Noble GTO. A 2003 M12 GTO is shown here.

Glossary

aerodynamic: having a shape that improves airflow around a car to increase its speed

all-wheel drive: a system of moving a car that powers all four wheels instead of just the front or back wheels

alternator: a car part that works with the battery to make electrical power

concept car: a car built to show a new design and features that may one day be used in cars sold to the public

convertible: a car with a roof that can be lowered or removed

coupe: a two-door car with one section for the seat and another for storage space

cylinder: a tube-shaped space in an engine in which moving parts use air and fuel to create power

designer: one who plans the pattern or shape of something

exhaust: a passage through which gases escape from a car or motorcycle

grille: a metal screen on the front of a car that allows cool air into the engine

muscle car: a midsize sports car with a powerful engine built for speed

pony car: a small, affordable car with a sporty image

speedometer: an instrument that measures distance and speed

spoiler: a wing-shaped device attached to the back of the car to improve airflow and stability

wind tunnel: a tunnel in which a current of air is blown around a car to determine its aerodynamic qualities

For More Information

Books

Bradley, Michael. *GTO*. New York, NY: Marshall Cavendish Benchmark, 2010.

Zuehlke, Jeffrey. *Muscle Cars*. Minneapolis, MN: Lerner Publications Company, 2007.

Web Sites

Collisionkids.org
www.collisionkids.org
Learn about cars by playing games and completing related projects.

Ferraris
www.ferrari.com
Check out Ferrari GTO history, other Ferraris, and the latest Ferrari news.

GTO Association of America
www.gtoaa.org
Get technical advice and more information about Pontiac GTOs.

Index